THOUGHTS ALIVE

Your Power to Happiness

Cindy Wahlberg

THOUGHTS ALIVE

Your Power to Happiness

By Cindy Wahlberg

Published By
Positive Imaging, LLC
bill@positive-imaging.com

All Rights Reserved

Early Praise For Thoughts Alive

5 Stars

I now realize that we do create our own happiness.

Truth, Inspirational an Eye opener! A must read for all.. I now realize that We do create our own happiness, Thanks Cindy!

5 Stars

Inspirational Soul Searching

From the beginning to the end this book focuses on what life is and how YOU control it. It is a very inspirational, soul searching and even more a realization of your control to life and living it.

5 Stars

Inspiring and thought provoking. Highly recommend!

Great book! Very uplifting! Amazing positive information to use everyday,to make great changes to your life! Thank you Cindy.

Special Thanks

Thank you to "My Husband," and sons Nolan and Crosby. I thank you for all your love and support and understanding on this amazing new journey. I could not have done it without you.

To my father, Maurice. The best dad a girl could ever ask for. Although you are now non-physical, your love and encouragement during the creation of this book, from beginning to end, will never be forgotten.

Thank you to Bill Benitez and Positive Imaging, LLC Publishing. You went above and beyond anything I ever expected. Thank you for your knowledge, expertise, patience, and diligence.

Thank you to all mentioned or not in this book, you have touched my life in more ways than you will ever know.

All My Love,

Cindy

Contents

Like a tree growing through a rock, anything is possible. We can be, do, and have anything we want in our life. Knowing, believing, trusting...this is where your power lies.

You are a Powerful Creator!

~CW

Introduction

Keep reminding yourself: I get what I think about, whether I want it or not.

~ *Dr. Wayne Dyer*

I write this book for you, the ones who wake up every day and question life. Who feel there must be more, more out there, more to this life. There must be more than the monotonous day to day living. Working, home life, kids, routines, bills, schedules and responsibilities. Who feel they are going through the motions of life, but not really living. Who feel a void, know they want something, but are not sure where to go or how to start. For those who are living the day to day grind of life and still struggle every day, just to get by. Who sacrifice, lack energy, who simply feel numb. There must be more...

I write this book for you, to share with you my Journey. What I have learned, what I have discovered. The Truth and Power of who We Truly are.

Some of you may be hearing this for the first time in your life. For some, it may simply break things down to a clearer, deeper understanding. I write this with Love and Truth. *This is Your Answer to True Happiness.*

1

What If

Energy cannot be created or destroyed; it can only be changed from one form to another.

~ Albert Einstein

What if you woke up and learned that you are the Creator of Your World? That you could now, today, control EVERYTHING that happens to you and EVERYTHING that comes to you? That you could create everything in your life? That you could simply think a certain way and things that you wanted came right into your existence? Whatever you wanted? Anything, any life experience, any lifestyle, any journey? That any wish you had would come true? No matter what the wish. What if you had all the Powers of the World in You? That you were Queen or King of your world? What if you had your very own Genie in a lamp with Unlimited Wishes, for Eternity? What if everything you have ever wished for, wanted and desired was yours? How would what you thought about change? What would you do next? How would you feel? What would your dreams look like? How would you spend your day? Would you focus any longer on the things you didn't want? Those bills? That boss? That problem?

What if I told you, the real reason you feel so strongly about wanting more, of having more and feel so frustrated when you don't get what you want and desire, is because deep down, you know you SHOULD have more, that you CAN have more, that you DESERVE to have more?

What if I told you that you CHOSE to be here, Alive, here on this Earth, to experience life? To have adventures, creating your wishes and desires, while having fun along the way? That you deserve nothing but HAPPINESS? AND that you can have it ALL!

What if I told you that <u>YOU</u> are the only person who can control what is created in your experience? That you DO deserve and are worthy of Everything you have ever wanted in your life.

I am here to tell you, The answer is YES!!!!! You Can Have Anything you want, you can be anything you want, and you can do anything you want. AND you can start Right Now! Start right at THIS very moment. You can have any wish you have ever wanted. And it is so Simple and all in YOUR control. Our Thoughts are so, so, so, much more powerful than anyone has ever led us to believe. Our Thoughts are Alive, they are Alive and so powerful that what you are thinking right now is actually creating your future. YES, you read that right... YOUR

THOUGHTS ARE ALIVE!!! YOUR THOUGHTS CREATE!!!

This book will help you "re-member" who you really are and just how powerful you truly are. YOU are UNIVERSAL ENERGY! YOU are Non-Physical Energy, A SOUL having a Human Experience. Eternal Energy, in Human Form. Do You Understand What this Means!? This is flipping around everything that we have Ever Known, everything we have ever thought about life. Go Back and Re-Read that to absorb and comprehend this just a little more. That Is a Pretty Heavy Sentence, hard to swallow, but **100% True!**

YOU are UNIVERSAL ENERGY! YOU are, Non-Physical Energy, A SOUL having a Human Experience. Eternal Energy, in Human Form.

You never cease to exist... We talk about being human and having a Soul, but it's the other way around. *WE ARE A SOUL*. We are being human (physical) here and now. Experiencing life on Earth.

Allow yourself to take a deep breath, to absorb this a bit further. Deeper. Imagine. Daydream. Release some tension, some stress, some worry... Feel calm... Let go a little bit more and maybe even Smile. The truth is, *YOU ARE FREE!*

Your life, this experience, did not just happen by chance. You chose to come here. You chose to be born, to have this physical human, body experience. You chose to experience life. To SEE, To TOUCH, To SMELL, to TASTE, and To HEAR Your Physical World!

Think about this... How do you feel when you are sitting in a restaurant, waiting with excited anticipation for your meal to come? How absolutely excited, over the moon are you when you take that first bite into your favorite food? How does it taste? How about when you have been hungry for a long while? How does it smell? How does it make you feel?

How does it feels when you are out in nature, at the ocean, out in the rain, near a waterfall or hear a bird chirping? Sitting with your face to the sun? That warm bright sunshine warming you to your core. Doesn't it make you feel calm and peaceful? Less stressed? More clear minded? More, dare I say, "centered?"

How about when you first fall in love? Deep feelings overcome your heart, you become light on your feet, you feel happy all the time, on cloud nine, carefree. A permanent smile is pasted on your face. You can spend all day and night with that person, talking all through the night, never feeling sleep deprived, still full of energy even with little to no sleep.

Or, think about how quenching and delicious is it when you finally get a drink after being thirsty for a long period of time? On a hot summer day? How does that first sip taste? Cold, refreshing? Quenching? Satisfying?

What about when you have an orgasm...How does it feel? That amazing jolt of glorious sensation through your entire body...

That's why you came! It's these Feelings, these Amazing Sensations. You came To FEEL THIS PHYSICAL WORLD! **To Feel Alive**! That is why you chose to be here in your flesh and bony body. You came to experience and feel life! And, when you have felt the negativity of being thirsty for a long time, that very first sip is better, more satisfying than if you were never thirsty at all.

Some people are much more "in tune" with their non-physical side than others. We usually label them as 'sensitive', or 'intuitive'. Some are our healers of the world. Mothers are especially "in tune." We know when something's really wrong, we feel it, we know. We know when the cry is nothing to worry about, and when we need to worry. We just "know." It's our "gut feeling." But we are all energy, we all have this innate ability, whether you know it, believe it or not. It's who we are.

I always knew what part of the house my boys were in when I could not see them. Whether they were upstairs, on the other side of the house, outside or just in the next room, I don't know how, but I just knew. I could feel the energy, their presence. That is our non-physical side. We "feel" the energy.

The truth is We are FREE! We have all the freedom in the world. We never need to fear, worry or be intimidated by the unknown. We came to create! We came to be Alive! We came to experience Life! That is ALL and that is EVERYTHING!!

This is the truth of our existence and the truth of how we create our lives. I write this for You. For you, so you may know this Truth that has been unknown to us for far too long.

The soul is here for its own joy ~ Rumi

Reflections

To clarify, you are non-physical energy having a human experience. You are a Soul. You are having a physical experience. We are all Kings and Queens of our own lives. You chose to come here, to be born, to experience life, to feel life through all your senses. To be physical in this physical world. You came to feel, to touch, taste, to smell and to hear. To feel "Alive." To feel everything in this "physical world." Your thoughts are Alive and your thoughts create! When you have any negative in your life, please know that it's ok. Negative feelings are still feelings, it's still a physical feeling and they make the positive experiences in your life so much more. You are in control of your own destiny. All the powers of the world are in all of us. We can and have created our world, thought by thought, everything in our lives. You can live the life of your dreams, whatever those dreams may be, you can have it. We all deserve and are worthy of everything and anything that we have ever wanted and desired in our lives. This knowledge, this power in You, is how you begin to create your life on purpose, how to intentionally create your life.

2

We are Creators

"What you think, you become. What you feel, you attract. What you imagine, you create."

~Buddha

We are creators of our own lives. The reason why you feel so much negative emotion, anger, resentment, bitterness or disappointment when you are stopped from having what it is you truly want, from being or doing what you truly desire is because you know, deep down, that you should be able to create, to wish and have all that you dream of. Deep down, you know your Power, you know your truth and you subconsciously expect the freedom to choose. You know and feel who you truly are and why you came here. You can feel it in your gut. You CAN create your own life, your own desires, and your own destiny! You can have it All!

Think back to your early memories of being a young child. Do you remember how you spent your days exploring your world? You loved being the center of everyone's attention. You loved life and everything in it. You played and laughed and smiled, imagined and daydreamed all day, every day. You went from one fun thing to another and another, never running out of fun. You imagined and played out your dreams and fantasies. You reveled in trying new things, seeing, touching, hearing and smelling everything you could in your world. Try and think back to how free, lighthearted and happy you felt. You were the center of your world. You knew your power then, you knew your worthiness. You knew who you truly are.

But, once you grew a bit older and went to school, you began having to follow rules. Structure and routine started. You had to conform more, do as you're told more, pay attention more, daydreaming and imagining less. You were ordered to "stop acting like a child." Told "how immature you were acting," "told to act your age." Do you remember how angry you felt? You felt utter disbelief, frustration, and irate, when you were told no, when you couldn't do something you wanted to do or have something that you wanted. You became enraged at anyone who yelled or ridiculed you. Think back to how negative you felt, how flustered and angry you became so quickly. How easily you became agitated and sometimes nearing a total melt down, or threw a tantrum. You knew...

As you got older and became a young adult you were "taught" (by family, teachers and neighbors who did not know their own power) that you were not special, that you should not have a big ego, to not be selfish, to stop and face "reality." Told that you must be like everyone else, to not think for yourself. To follow the rules. That you must do what you're told, and to never, ever question authority.

Why do you think everyone can't wait to be an adult?!? We spend our childhood and teen years yearning to be a grown up! It's because we can't wait for the freedom to choose how we live. The freedom to do what we want. The freedom to live our life as we wish. But, by the time we become an adult we have forgotten that we are free! Forgotten that we are the creator of our own lives. So, Instead of "finally" having the freedom we wish for, we give it up to bosses and landlords, mortgage companies, debtors. To the city we live, to the economy, to the government. We become enslaved, not knowing our Power.

You have God Power in you. Your Thoughts are how you Create. No matter what you may currently believe, this is true for every Human on Earth. No matter what you may have been told, no matter what religion you are. This is Universal Law!

It's written in the Bible as well

John 10:34 *Jesus answered them, it is not written in your law, I said You are Gods!*

We are God of our own life! That is what Jesus was saying! We create our lives, we are creators! And we do this by our thoughts.

Matthew 21:21 Jesus replied, Truly I tell you, if you have Faith and Do Not Doubt, not only can YOU do what was done to the fig tree, but also, YOU can say to this mountain, "GO, Throw Yourself into the Sea", And It Will Be Done.

All of the Powers of the World are in You! You are GOD of your own life. YOU came to experience your life! To have fun, to experience all the delicious adventures in your life that You create. You didn't come here to just pay bills, be stressed out, have high anxiety or be zombies of routine. You came to feel the physical world! To create your life! You, my dear friend, have God Power in you. You can and have created your world. Your life has unfolded just as you have thought it into being, all the good, the bad and the ugly! It was all created by you. It's time to remember this and as each new event and circumstance comes up in your life, before you react with anger, fear, resentment, jealousy, trepidation, or any other negative feelings or thoughts, remember this...

Give yourself a moment to breathe, to pause and take this in. Please know that you have lost nothing and have gained Everything! All is well and *Everything* always works out for you, Always! Always Believe this! You are Free!

Many years ago I read "The Secret" by Rhonda Byrne, watched the movie, and delved into the study of the Law of Attraction. I was so excited and thought, "OK, I got this." Ask, Believe, Receive. It's like electricity, we don't understand how it works, but "you can cook a meal with it, and you can cook a man with it." I am sure if you read about or studied the Law of Attraction, you got as excited and pumped up as I did. For a while, I expected to see everything I wished for just come falling out of the sky all at once... But, in the back of my mind, I doubted it could be real, it seemed farfetched. Until one day, five years later, it hit me. My family and I were sitting on the floor in our new apartment in Austin, Texas. We had just arrived. We had left everything behind on the East Coast and as we sat there, we wondered out loud how on Earth we did it. How did we get here? We were dumbstruck as to how we were able to pull it off. We were in TEXAS! We literally had no way of getting there and starting over, BUT WE DID! And in that moment, I got it. I realized, everything that I had wanted five years prior had been manifested. Everything I desired or wished for came true. For instance, I had wanted to work in the Health Industry and study Holistic Health. I wanted to move to a warm climate, a green conscious city, a musical town, with great schools, close to Universities and lots of culture. Well, in those five years, I lost my sales job in publishing; enrolled in a Holistic Health College with my severance pay from that job. I met the Human Resources Director of a local hospital. Became good friends with her, (simply by chance) and within a month or two of meeting her, I was working in the medical industry. Oh, and of course, the biggest one, we moved to Austin Texas, The Live Music Capital of the World. Everything came to me to fulfill each one of my wishes, even losing a great job and thought at the time was the worst thing that could happen to myself and my family. But really it was just bringing me to my next wish. I didn't realize that I was creating it, until I looked back, even moving halfway across the country. *Now, I know, Nothing, Absolutely Nothing, is Impossible, as long as you Trust, Let Go and Believe.*

I realize now, all the negative things we were experiencing in our lives, the things we did not want back then, the stresses in our lives, the worries, it all helped us to know, without a doubt what it was that we really truly wanted. If we were satisfied with our lives at the time or happy where we were living, then we would not have had that strong wanting for something different. So negativity is not really a bad thing. Without it, you would never know what is truly meaningful to you. Think back to what I wrote in the first chapter. When you take that first sip of water after being thirsty for so long, that first sip tastes <u>phenomenal</u>. It's the most quenching, the best tasting drink, you have had, better than if you were never thirsty at all.

Reflections

We are Gods of our own life. You have God Power in you. We are the creators of our world, our lives, and we create through our thoughts. It is Universal Law. Day by day, thought by thought we are creating each aspect, every detail of our life. We chose to come here to create. We came to have fun, to experience all the delicious adventures in our life that we have manifested. We came to feel the physical world, to simply feel Alive! You can create right now, the perfect life for <u>you</u>. Absolutely nothing is impossible as long as you believe. The Universe Loves you and always has your back. Take a deep breath, feel the calm and ease in you, release all tensions, feel the unconditional love for you from the Universe. You are Loved! You are Free!

3

THOUGHTS ALIVE

Philippians 2:5 - Let this mind be in you, which was also in Christ Jesus

Because our Thoughts are Alive, as we think, live our day to day lives, worry, fear, daydream and imagine, we are creating our future. You can and have created your world. Your life has unfolded just as you have thought it to be. Step, by step, thought by thought, it was all created, manifested by you. You just didn't know it. So instead of creating what you wanted, you were creating what you were seeing, what was around you, what you were experiencing at that time, what you believed you could have and could not create what you thought you couldn't have. We just weren't aware, so without knowing it, we have been creating our lives by default, on auto-pilot, without knowing that it was always in our own control.

Your thoughts are Alive, your thoughts are Energy. The truth is You can think *anything* into being. You can have any lifestyle. You can live any way you wish. No matter what it is. Whether it's the vacation you want to go on, more money in your bank account, the perfect job, the perfect relationship, a successful business, a perfect fit body, a perfectly healthy body, or if you just want to sit on a beach all day, or any other dream or desire you wish. You can have anything you want. You can be anything you want to be. Maybe you just want less stress and more calmness in your life. When you start to Talk about what you want, you bring it to you. Talk about your body healing and it will heal, talk about being thin (never the opposite) and you will become thin. Talk about having money and money will come to you. Talk about the job that you want and you will get it. Talk about the person you wish to meet and that person will appear. Envision the place you want to be, and you will get there. The thoughts you think determines everything in your life. As you turn your attention (what you are thinking) towards what you want to see in your world, that is what you will see in your life. You get to have it all! You are your own artist. Your thoughts are the paintbrush! Your life, the canvas. AND nothing is impossible!

The Universe is always listening, but, it does not hear what you want, not in words. It feels through vibration, through energy, through frequencies what you want, what you feel. As long as you do not doubt and you believe, the Universe will show it to you. It's a knowing you can feel in your gut.

Test it. Tell the Universe what it is that you want to see and then look for the signs. Ask to hear a song or see your favorite movie. Ask for a bird, a flower, a rainbow, a $20 bill, or an unexpected cup of coffee. Whatever you want. Start with something small, something you believe you can have. It may take an hour it may take 48 hours but it will come. Feel it coming to you and believe, but don't think about how it will come, just know that it will. That is how powerful you truly are. Be easy about it. Be calm. Don't force it and most importantly have fun!

In the winter of 2009, I was laid off from my sales job. That following spring, I really wanted to buy a pool for our backyard. However, with two young boys, a mortgage, and two car payments, having only one income made it impossible. They were selling for about $2000-$4,000 at that time. I remember we were still reeling from the "Great Recession" and had no idea when or if I would find another job. On a very warm, sunny day, I sat outside in our back-yard. My bare feet in the grass, eyes closed, my face facing the sun. I started daydreaming. As I drifted deeper into the dream, I saw a swimming pool in our back yard. I could feel the pool right next to me. In those few moments, it felt so real that if I reached out I could touch it. As I opened my eyes I thought "WHOA!" "That was amazing!" It felt so real. In that moment, we no longer needed a pool, in those few seconds, we had one. It felt like a trance.

Forty-eight hours later, while drinking my morning coffee, not looking for anything in particular, I scanned through our local paper. To my surprise, I found someone selling a metal above ground pool. It was a large oval twelve foot x twenty-four foot x four foot pool. They included EVERYTHING, All the accessories, from the ladder to the chemicals, toys, bricks, skimmers, filters, the cover, everything we would need but the water and sand. And, it was only $600. Within a week, we had a pool in our backyard just like I had envisioned. I had no idea then, but I created that pool. I thought it into being and didn't even know it. And the best part, it was easy and fun!

Reflections

Our Thoughts are Alive. Every thought you think is alive and creates your life. You just didn't know it. You have been creating your life, without knowing that it was always in your own control.

Your thoughts are Alive and create your life. You can create any lifestyle, any dream or desire you wish. You can have it All. Anything... You can have whatever you wish. You can create anything in your life. You have the power, <u>you</u> hold the power. The Universe is always listening and loves you unconditionally. Nothing is impossible! This is how powerful you truly are. Be easy about it and have fun!

4

The Law of Attraction

As far as I can tell, it's just about letting the Universe know what you want and working toward it, while letting go of how it might come to pass.

~Jim Carrey

The Law of Attraction is a Universal Law, just like the Law of Gravity. It's not something that is real only if you hear about it, and it's not something that's new. It's as old as time and as predictable as gravity.

The Law of Attraction says "like attracts like." And the attraction comes to you in the way of your thoughts. Whatever you think about, whether you want it or you do not want it, the Law of Attraction (LOA) will find you a match for that thought each and every time. Think of your thoughts as a magnet, whatever you think about is what will come to you, no matter what the thought is. No matter whether it is good or bad, wanted or unwanted, the Law of Attraction doesn't decipher. Just like the Law of Gravity doesn't decipher whether you are a good person, bad person, young or old, homeless or a millionaire. No matter what the reason or circumstance you will never ever fall up, if you fall off a building and no matter the object, a feather or a two-ton truck, it will always fall down. The Law of Attraction (LOA) works exactly the same way. The Law of Attraction will find a match to whatever it is you are thinking and will bring you more of it. By making sure your thoughts are focused more on "what you want" and less on what you do not want is a *very crucial step* in creating your life on purpose.

There are many great people, inventors, and celebrities in this world who know this power and have used this knowledge to create all the success in their lives; Albert Einstein, Nikola Tesla, Andrew Carnegie, Ralph Waldo Emerson, Henry Ford, Walt Disney, Denzel Washington, Matt Damon, Oprah Winfrey, Will Smith, Russell Brand, Steve Harvey, and Jim Carrey, to name just a few. Have you ever watched a video of Jim Carrey? He carried a ten-million dollar check in his pocket that he wrote to himself five years before his first film. Or what about Oprah, she used the Law of Attraction and didn't even know it to get the part in "The Color Purple."

You don't become what you want, you become what you believe.

~ Oprah Winfrey

Have you ever bought something, brought it home and then all you saw were people with that very same thing? As soon as you got it, you began to see it everywhere you went? You noticed people talking about it, saw commercials on T.V. and saw signs all over about it? You were in complete shock because you thought what you brought home was so unique and different when you bought it? Thought you were the only one. That's not your imagination, that's the Law of Attraction at work. It's not complicated, but does require you to do a complete 180 degree turn on how you think. Everything you are thinking is creating. The Universe is matching that thought that you are thinking and every feeling you have is telling you if your creation is positive or negative, good or bad. And the best part of all of this is, you now can control everything that comes to you by noticing what you are thinking. Start paying attention to your thoughts and you will see what you are attracting. Pay attention to what you say throughout your day. Do you say negative things, and in return bring those negative situations to you? Things like, "I know there will be a lot of traffic today" or "today is going to suck," or "I always get stuck at that light" or "that coworker always makes me angry" or "I never find a good seat" or whatever. Every time you think a thought like these, the universe is saying, ok, here is a match to what you just said and oh, here is more of that. It is bringing to you exactly what you do not want. It's what you expect, but NOT what you want.

You will begin to notice it in others as well. You'll hear conversations and comments like, "Oh that always happens to me" or "with my luck..." or "I always get sick when…" Start saying to yourself instead, "WOW" everything always works out for me and "Oh, Life is so wonderful!" "Everything comes to me so easily!" I always get the best… (Fill in the blank). When you change what you expect to come to you, you change what comes to you.

Do you know someone who is always winning stuff? Any game they play, contest they enter, they always win? No matter what game, place, situation or scenario, they always win. Whether it's a new car, money, a cup of coffee or a trip somewhere, they are always winning? They are using the Law of Attraction and may not even know it. They simply feel lucky and don't resist it.

When my boys were little they looked so much a like people thought they were twins. They both had blue eyes and blonde hair and were pretty close in age. Everywhere we went people would come up to us, ask if they were twins, comment about how adorable they were and how similar their appearance was. They got so much attention from strangers every place we went. Even at a very young age they automatically responded when asked if they were twins, "no, we are eighteen months apart" they would say in unison. It was astounding the attention they got. It wasn't until after I had them that I began to notice how many other young blonde hair, blue eyed babies and toddlers were living near us. I never noticed them before. Suddenly that was all I saw, it was truly amazing. At the park, at their school, at the bank, at the supermarket, at the beach, everywhere we went every day. It was as if they had a blonde hair blue eyed burst where we lived when they were born. They were everywhere. Yet, the attention that they received from strangers was as if they were the only ones in existence. This went on for many years. My husband and I even became friends with a couple who had blonde hair, blue eyed twin girls.

As the boys got older, they started to receive less and less attention. At the same time, I stopped noticing those little blonde haired blue eyed toddlers around me as well. I just didn't see them anymore, it was as if they were no longer around, or they all just disappeared all at once. We stopped focusing on it, as they got older, our thoughts and focus changed, changing the energies focus (blonde hair blue eyed babies and toddlers) to a different focus. SO as our thoughts changed, what we started seeing and living changed.

When we moved into our new home, I brought a puppy home, a chocolate lab named Shiloh. That very same day, we started seeing little Shiloh's everywhere we went. I saw chocolate labs all over! I really never paid much attention to Labrador's at all until I brought him home. But, boom, there they were! I never noticed that I had 2 neighbors in our neighborhood that had a chocolate and another near my parent's home. They were in cars as we drove by, at the park, in pet stores and running on the beach. It was truly remarkable.

The day we bought a new white car, we pulled into the supermarket parking lot on our way home. Instantly my jaw dropped, and I said out loud, "holy cow!" do you see all the white cars in the parking lot?!? The parking lot was completely filled with white cars with just a splash of other colors. That's the law of attraction working. Since I was focused on our new white car that was all I saw.

As I began to learn about the Law of Attraction and how it really works, I realized that I can control my thoughts and with that, begin to control what is brought to me. I began to have some fun with it. I started by deciding to find a heart while I took a walk one day. Something simple, something easy. Not only did I find a heart shaped leaf, I also found a rock that was in a perfect heart shape. Shortly after, a car drove by with red and pink hearts splattered all over it. I was absolutely blown away. Now, I see hearts everywhere I go.

Just before we left for our journey across the country, to Austin, Texas, my sister gave me a small Buddha Statue that had belonged to our Aunt. It was small enough to fit in my pocket, so I took it with me everywhere I went. I called it my "Happy Buddha" and each time I pulled it out I would name something that made me happy. I always smiled when I looked at it and kept it under my pillow at night while I slept. Sometimes though, I would forget about where I left it and would lose it. But, I always knew the last place I had it and found it within a day or two. After about six months in Texas, I lost it. I looked everywhere for it, tore apart bedding and boxes, searched clothes piles, my car, work desk, pocketbook, and furniture. I searched high and low, every place I could think of, to no avail. I was very upset by this. Every few days or weeks I would begin my search again. This went on for many weeks maybe months. After a very long while, I finally gave up and succumbed to the realization that it was gone forever. However every now and then, I would find myself searching again. I really, really wanted to find it! I loved it and wanted it back, it was really very important to me.

One day, many months later, after reading about energy, thought power and mind creation, I decided that I have all the powers of the universe in me and I would not take no for an answer. I was determined to find my "Happy Buddha". I wanted it back and *demanded* that the Universe show it to me within forty-eight hours. Well, the Universe has quite a sense of humor, because in exactly forty-eight hours from the moment I declared that it show itself to me, I walked into our home to find my boys tearing apart our entire apartment in search of Nolan's bearded dragon. I completely freaked out. We tore the entire apartment upside down. Every shelf, every box, every couch cushion, every piece of clothing. Every object we owned was dumped out onto the floor. After many, many, hours of searching all through the night, we were just about to give up. I walked back into my bedroom, opened a box with my husband's belongings in it (on his side of the closet) and there, under a full box of "stuff" was my Buddha at the very bottom underneath everything else! How it got in there, I will never know. I am not supposed to know. What I can tell you though, is that we did not find the lizard that day. It came out on its own a few days later. But I was so utterly dumbstruck, with what had occurred.

I DID IT! That was MY power! It was MY mind, MY thoughts that brought it back to me. Wow! It really truly does work!

This story is one of the main reasons why I am writing this book for you. This is what I want everyone to know. This is how Powerful our thoughts are. This is how powerful you are! It really is true! It really does work and my Buddha is my proof of that! Now go and use **YOUR** Power, **Your** Thoughts, **Your** Mind to create what it is YOU *really truly want!*

Reflections

The Law of Attraction is a Universal Law. Just like the Law of Gravity, it is a powerful and impartial law. The Law of Attraction says like attracts like and comes to you by your thoughts. Whatever you are thinking (anything you are thinking) the Universe will find a match to that thought and bring you more of it. Whatever you think about, whether you want it or not. Always, Every time, no matter what the reason or circumstance. Your thoughts are like a magnet, whatever you think about is what will come to you. By making sure your thoughts are focused more on "what you want" and less on what you do not want, by paying attention to your thoughts is a *crucial step* in creating your life on purpose.

5
Positive vs Negative Thoughts

Choosing to be positive and having a grateful attitude is going to determine how you're going to live your life.

~Joel Osteen

In our society we tend to focus ALL of our energy talking, complaining and telling everyone within ear shot all the negative things that happens to us each day. Everything that has made us angry, annoyed, pissed off and upset. Everything that we do not want to see in our life is what we focus on the most. So, by default, we keep creating everything that we do not want in our lives. Over and over again, we complain, bitch, moan and complain some more. We tell everyone we know about all the things that happen in our life that makes us angry. We can't wait to share all the gruesome details with our friends, spouses, siblings, neighbors, and co-workers. We tell the same story over and over again to each person we talk to and express, in great detail, all the gruesome injustices that are done to us. We talk about it, we blog about it, we text about it, we rant about it, post and share about it. Little do we know that with each negative thing we talk about, The Universe finds a match, and again, there is more negative to talk about, rinse and repeat. It goes on and on. Day after day, week after week, year after year. Instead of getting what we want, we continue getting what we do not want. And as such, we continue to ask why our lives are the way they are.

One of the most vital things that you can do right here, right now, is to stop any and all negative talk. *This is your job now.* Your job, is to pay attention to your thoughts and each time you are thinking a negative thought, find something, **anything,** to take your mind off of it and onto something positive, something good, something that you WANT to see in your life. Remember, what you are seeing and experiencing in your life right now are your past thoughts, it's old news. Now that you are aware of this, now that you know this and understand, you now have control over your future. You know Your Power now. All of your freedom is in knowing your power. As long as you control your thoughts you have all the freedom in your world. You control everything.

If you want something in your life to change, then you must start to think of positive outcomes, positive dreams, and positive desires to make your future what you want it to be. Picture your future how you wish it to be. Happiness is the answer to it all, it's the answer to everything that you want now or will ever want. If at any time it becomes uncomfortable, if you start to feel angry, hesitant, scared or feel any other negative feeling, or if what you are thinking, you begin to doubt, if you start to believe that it is not possible, then STOP immediately and find another thought. Don't think about that thing you do not want at all, don't think about anything that doesn't feel good. Change your thinking right away. This is where your freedom lies. By learning to control your thoughts, you control your world.

In the beginning, it will take a bit of effort, you will really have to be aware and stop your negative thoughts and switch your thoughts to something happier, something positive, things wanted. We are so programmed to think negative, to worry and doubt, that it will be a challenge at first. But just as with anything new you try, like dieting and exercising or quitting smoking, with practice, it will get easier and easier as the days go on. After a little while, you will become aware quicker, catch yourself thinking negatively sooner. What will begin to happen is you will start to notice that more positive situations and outcomes will begin to come to you. You'll start to find more "good days" where everything goes right, where everything works out with less effort, more ease.

Begin thinking, dreaming and talking about the things that make you happy, the things that you want to see in your life. Talk about your desires, aspirations, write about them, think about them, dream about them, daydream about what you love and what you wish for. Reach for happy thoughts, happy moments, whatever feels good to think about. Guide your thoughts to happy memories and future outcomes. Get Happy! Or, if that seems too difficult at first, if you have a hard time stopping the negative feeling, or have a hard time holding onto your positive feelings, then just start to change your thoughts to something else, something completely off that subject, until your negative feelings dissipate. This will make a tremendous difference in your life. Just be easy on yourself, know that you are learning a new way of thinking, a new way of living. You're flipping around everything you have ever known, everything that you have ever thought to be true. Everything that you have ever lived. It's a complete one hundred eighty degree turn around of thinking. Just know that you got this! You are powerful! You are loved! You are a Powerful Creator!

By knowing this, you are Free. You are free to think how you think. You and only you control what you think, how you think. All of your freedom is in changing your thoughts. In guiding them where you want them to be. All of your freedom is in **your** power. As long as You can guide your thoughts, you are always free.

I use a phrase I read a few years back. Well, I "altered" it a bit to keep it positive. It helps me to remember to keep things simple, to be easier on myself. To relax, not to rush things, to know that everything is coming to me with ease.

KISS- Keep It Simple Sunshine! I love it. I say this every day to myself out loud and when I notice that I am pushing to make something happen or to help me make a decision. I immediately stop and say "Keep it simple sunshine!"

Keep it simple. We make things so complicated. Everything we do becomes a process. Steps to be taken, plans laid out, goals to be set. No pain, no gain. If you're not moving, you're lazy. Work hard, play harder. We have it all mixed up. Instead, we need to relax, think positive, happy thoughts and let the good come to us.

When my son Crosby turned 7 years old, we brought home this adorable little puppy. Shiloh was Nolan's dog, so we wanted Crosby to have his own dog. When the dog owner handed "Toby" over to us, he said, *"Good Luck"*...we were puzzled by this, but really didn't pay much attention. It wasn't more than twenty-four hours that we started to realize what the owner meant. Toby, while absolutely cute and so darn adorable, was getting into mischief every chance he got. He kept jumping out of the car window each time the car would stop, he closed the window on his neck with his paw a few times choking himself as well. He chewed up our bathroom rug, many of the boy's toys and stuffed animals, our ottoman, and even our brand new coffee table. He began getting out of the gate in our backyard, continuously barking at our next door neighbors on their porch. He then started running across busy intersections. Each time he did something wrong, we talked about it. We started sharing stories with everyone about this "bad" new puppy we had. We told family, shared stories with our neighbors and friends. Every day, it seemed we had a new story to share and, with each new day, Toby got bigger and bigger and so did his mischiefs. Not only was he tearing things apart, but he started fighting with our neighbor's animals. It got so bad that one of our neighbors called the police on him for scratching her dog. Another incident, a neighbor's dog attacked him and ripped off part of Toby's ear, leaving them both quarantined for a month by the SPCA. We were fired by a professional dog sitter, the owner of the company stating she had such a hard time with him, he took up so much time and she just did not want to come back. He killed our neighbor's cat when it jumped our fence into our yard. And the absolute worst, he killed one of our neighbor's brand new puppy.

The problems with Toby just got bigger and bigger and each time something happened, we talked, complained and fussed about it. We thought with each new incident that we would have to get rid of him. And with each new incident, we tried to fix the problem but the problem was still always the problem.

Fast forward five years to when we were moving to Austin and we really were concerned. We had to drive with him for two days. We had no idea how he would be on the trip, stuck in the back of our van and seeing other animals at rest stops. We didn't think it would go well and we were moving to an apartment complex that was full of other dogs and cats. We were terrified.

BUT what happened instead was an absolute miracle. Toby was a perfect angel on the two-day road trip. He was relaxed, (as were we) quiet, he listened very well and loved being in the van with us. Once we arrived, we started talking about how good he was and less about the stories of horror. Slowly, Toby became a really good dog. He started to listen better, was calm and very well behaved. Little by little, our timing became so good that we hardly ever ran into other neighbors. As time went on we rarely would see any other animals outside or Toby just simply ignored them. He even found a human friend that loved him, stopped just to pet and talk to him daily, and often gave him tennis balls for him to play with when he saw him.

The reason I named this chapter "Positive vs Negative" is twofold. Number one, it is in your best interest, and probably one of the most important things that you can do *for you* right now is to STOP any and all negative talk! Right here, right now. What you need to do instead is start paying attention to your thoughts, start focusing on positive stories, positive outcomes, positive feelings, positive people, positive *everything*. This, I cannot find the words to explain how critical, how crucial this is, and how significantly this will affect your life. This is a huge, gigantic, tremendous, colossal step in changing your life, changing your outcomes, changing what comes to you. Once you start to change your thinking you will be blown away at how easily your life will transform. You will begin to create the life you have always wanted, desired, dreamed of. As you begin to practice daily, with each new day you will see more and more evidence of positive outcomes. More positive, happy situations, more coincidences, more days that just seem to have everything go right. When you realize that your thoughts are creating and that by just changing your thoughts, changes the outcome, and with that, changes your life, you then hold all the Power. Things that used to be a major ordeal will no longer be so. You are in control now, and now, when you do see negative come to you in your life you will not look at it with the same overwhelming dread and fear. You are a powerful creator, you are loved, you are free, you are magic!

However, if you only have positive life events, good happy outcomes in your life you would become bored, disinterested, blaśe, unenthused. You would not have things not wanted, difficult, or negative situations to help you decide what you want next. You would eventually stop creating. You need some negative in your life in order to know what you do not want, which in turn, forces you to know, in that moment, what it is you do truly want. Which then, helps you create your next desire. This is how life works. Now, you may be disagreeing with me right now, but if everything was perfect in your life you wouldn't have a *strong desire* to make anything else happen. If I didn't have a strong desire to move out of Delaware and didn't care about what was lacking in my life or my family's life, then I would have never found Austin. And if I didn't really have a strong desire to find my Buddha then I would not have looked so hard to find it or demanded that it be found. **AND** I probably would not have written this book!

When you meet that person who treats you bad, you immediately know that you want someone who treats you good. Being treated with kindness and respect now becomes a priority for you. You probably wouldn't have thought about it unless you had the negative. You then begin to daydream and wish for kindness, love, and appreciation, imagining the person of your dreams, the person who is caring, loving, understanding and compassionate (Although, if you keep going back to focusing on what was done to you, keep playing all the negative over and over again in your head, not letting it go, not forgetting and still focusing on what you do NOT want, then you will not be able to let in the positive). When you spend your days struggling, you wish for ease, for comfort. When you are fighting anything, you wish for peace. We would not know what is important, essential to us without having a strong negative thought about what we do not want or when living a negative situation. When you are ill you want wellness. When you are poor you want wealth.

Negative life events are not so scary when you realize that they are there to help you know what you really truly want in your life. Know that it's OK. Take a moment to take a deep breath and think about what it is you truly want. Think about what you want the outcome to be. Now you are creating your life as you wish.

Reflections

If you want something in your life to change, you must start to think of positive outcomes. Stop any and all negative thoughts and negative talk. Picture your future how you wish it to be. Talk about what makes you happy, think about and reach for happy thoughts, happy moments. Talk about your dreams, desires, aspirations, what you love and what you wish for. Whatever feels good to think about. Be easy on yourself. Get Happy! As you begin to practice daily, with each new day you will see more and more evidence of positive outcomes. You are in control now, and now, when you do see negative come to you in your life, you will not look at it the same way. Remember, in order to let positive in, you must be willing to let negative out.

BUT, You must have some negative in your life. This helps you to know what you do not want. Which in turn, forces you to know, in that moment, what it is you do want, which then helps you create your next desire. By knowing and understanding this, you now can remain calm, knowing that it's not bad, or the end of the world. You now know instantly what it is you want and can begin to create the outcome you desire. It's just your next creation.

6
Point of Focus

Our thoughts create our reality, where we put our focus is the direction we tend to go.
~ Peter McWilliams

Whatever you are thinking about or focusing on is called your Point of Focus. It's whatever you are looking at, paying attention to or giving your energy to. Your point of focus is what you are attracting to you. Whether it's positive or negative, wanted or unwanted. Whatever you think about, focus on, begins to expand, it gets bigger. Remember the Law of Attraction is going to find a match to your thoughts (your focus point) and give you more.

As you focus on a problem, the problem becomes your Point of Focus. Whatever it is, an illness, lack of money, a relationship, the person who makes you angry, your car, your job, your weight. Whatever it is, focusing on that problem will never change the scenario. The problem is still the focus. But, by simply changing your Point of Focus, by becoming aware of and taking control of your point of focus, by changing it to the outcome you want, what you want the resolution to be, you then change the situation. By simply taking your focus off of whatever the problem is, simply ignoring it, looking at something else altogether is enough for you to change your Focus Point.

Let's say, you are wanting to travel to a specific destination. Most of us would enter the location you want to get to into your GPS (Point of Focus), up pops a map of where you are now and the distance to the location you want to get to, your destination. The destination is now your new Focus Point. No matter how you get there or how long it takes, no matter what you pass along the way, your point of focus IS your destination. You control it. You can simply change your point of focus to where you want to be. Change your destination, the problem (WHAT YOU ARE FOCUSING ON) from where you are to the solution. Then the solution is what begins to show itself to you. This is why someone who is dieting and exercising begins to lose the weight. They are changing their focus to their slimming body, they start looking at themselves differently. They start seeing the positive results, Feeling the results. They begin feeling thin, focusing on a more positive outcome.

You want your point of focus to ALWAYS be what you want. You must always focus on the end result, where you want to be. You can control your point of focus by simply paying attention to what you are focusing on. Is it positive or negative? Once you begin to take notice of the differences, you will begin to catch yourself faster and faster AND gain better control. You'll begin to attract more positive situations, better outcomes and life experiences. You'll start to see with each new situation, issues and problems will begin to resolve themselves with more ease, less strain, and absolute calmness. You will get so good at catching yourself earlier and changing your thoughts, changing your Point of Focus. You'll begin to find that life will become easy, things will flow better, and your life will become magical and fun! *This is how you create on purpose!*

During our first few weeks living in Austin, I had a job interview and needed new "interview attire." We were pretty strapped for cash, but knew I needed to look the part to get the job. After the interview, we found that not only were we strapped for cash but we had a negative balance in our bank account and still needed to buy food and gas till payday. We needed something to make that happen. We decided the answer (solution) was to bring the clothes and shoes back that we had bought for the interview. We were pretty confident I had the job and knew in just a few weeks we could buy them again. The amount of returning the clothes would be just enough to get us until the end of the week. We had paid for everything with debit so we knew we would get the cash back. The first store we stopped at was no problem, we returned the clothes and got the cash back. When we arrived at the second store, however, we couldn't find the receipt, and, you know what that always means in retail, no receipt always equals store credit… Well, store credit was NOT going to help us, not one bit. So pretty strongly I affirmed without a doubt, we must have the cash, it's the only way! We went up to the register and explained our dilemma and as expected the cashier explained in perfect "retail lingo" the store policy, "no receipt equals, store credit only." Damn! BUT we NEEDED THE CASH! So the cashier ran the gift card through the machine and nothing happened! She tried again, still nothing. Again and again, she tried and then took out another gift card. She tried that one and another and another and each time the same thing, nothing. The machine wouldn't read the cards. She called her manager and explained what was happening. The manager told the cashier to re-boot the computer. As it was coming back online it dawned on me what was happening, this was the Universe working in our favor. I realized at that moment, that this was *my energy, my affirmation* and no amount of re-booting or trying new cards was going to get in the way. She tried a new box of gift cards that were un-opened, still, none of them worked. After about fifteen or twenty minutes at least twenty gift card attempts and a computer re-boot, we walked out with cash in hand! Now that is how powerful our thoughts really are!

Reflections

Your Point of Focus is whatever you are thinking about or focusing on. Whatever it is, positive or negative, wanted or unwanted, if you are focusing on it, it is getting bigger. As you focus on the problem, whatever the problem is, no matter what the situation, the problem is still your Point of Focus. As you continue to focus on the problem, the problem will continue to be, to exist. Focusing on it will never change the scenario. But, when you change your Point of Focus to the solution, then the solution is what begins to show itself to you. Your point of focus must ALWAYS be what you want the outcome to be. Always focus on the solution, the end result, the resolution, *what you want.* Or you can simply change your focus to a completely different subject altogether. Then the problem will disappear, it will just, stop-being. Once you begin to take notice of the differences, you'll start to see in your own life just how true this really is. You will begin to catch yourself faster and faster and you'll begin to see with each new situation, outcomes will begin to resolve themselves with more ease, less strain, and more calmness. You'll begin to attract more and more positive situations, outcomes and life experiences. This is how you create your life on purpose.

7
Feelings Matter

What you are Living is the Evidence of what you are Thinking and Feeling

~Abraham Hicks

How you feel is one of the most essential indicators of what you are creating. Your feelings are your gauge, they are letting you know what you are creating. When you feel negative emotions, any negative emotion, it means what you are creating is something not wanted. You can feel the negative on all levels of your being. Think of negative feelings as your warning light or check engine light on your car. That's your sign that what you are creating is not good. **Stop immediately** as soon as you feel any negative thoughts or feelings and calmly think a new thought. Change it, by focusing on what makes you feel good. Remember, you are in control now. You get to control what comes to you. When you are feeling good, happy and positive, you are creating in that moment, exactly what you want, you are creating what you have wanted, what you have asked for. When you find that positive feeling that feels good, hold onto it, milk it. Relax, take a deep breath and relish in those feel good feelings. Think those dreamy happy, amazing thoughts. Feel it. Soothe in it. Savor it. Keep thinking and daydreaming, those thoughts. Ask yourself every day, Am I Happy? If the answer is no, then stop and find a new happy thought.. Reach for and feel those good happy feelings. In that very moment, you can bring only happy, positive, good feeling situations to you. Only good can come to you. When you feel this way first, when you can feel happy and be positive first, then you are creating what you want.

Get picky about how you feel. Start each and every day happy, feeling good. Start to practice this every-day. When you choose happiness and positive feel-ings first, no matter what, with each new day, you will find that feeling good, feels better and that changing your thoughts and feeling good, gets easier. What ever you are wanting, looking for in your life, you want it because you know that having it will make you feel good. You want it to bring you happiness and your happiness makes you feel good. You want it because you know that feeling good, feels good. Feeling good first will bring what ever it is you want, to you. You may, with time, become a good feeling snob, not letting anyone get in your way of feeling good. It may sound selfish at first, but, if you are not happy, you will never ever be able to make anyone happy, ever. You know the saying "You cannot pour from an empty cup." Your cup must be filled with happiness in order to pour happiness onto others.

Decide with each new day that you will not accept any other feelings but good feelings, happy thoughts and watch your life transform. Play games, get creative and make it fun. When a Negative thought enters your mind, think of three Positive ones! Stop the negative thought right in its tracks. Train yourself to flip it around. Feel good first, be happy first, and love yourself first. It may sound silly, it may sound too simple, ridiculous, but doing this **will** change your life. Please know that you are going to be shocked, amazed, outrageously overjoyed at how your life will transform, you will be blown away! You ARE In Control!

Right around the year mark of our arrival to Texas, my husband and I became anxious and a bit negative. Up until this point, everything went our way, things just kind of fell into our lap, it was dream like, magical. We both found jobs quickly, both of us changed jobs twice, each for better positions and for better pay. Both of us were promoted within the first year, increasing our income further. We were able to get a loan and had a brand new car within 2 hours of searching. We found the perfect couch and loveseat set and had it delivered in perfect time of our guest's arrival. We even had a neighbor practically give us his 55-inch flat screen TV. We had just moved in, we had no furniture and only one TV had made the trip with us. There was a knock at the door. It was one of our new neighbors. He was leaving on a bus back to California. He was angry with his roommates, needed money and did not want to leave them the TV. He wanted us to buy the T.V. from him. We chuckled and showed him (jester-ring) our empty apartment and explained that we just arrived into town, had no furniture and no money. Our neighbor gave my husband the TV and was about to leave. What?!??! Seriously, it's a beautiful, practically brand new television. It was a fifty five inch Samsung flat screen. My husband ran to his wallet and gave him his last $40!

Once we hit that year mark, however, something happened. We both had it in our head, anticipated, expected, that once we were here, in Austin a year, we would be in a certain place. We would be better financially, more settled, have money in savings, that our apartment would be furnished more, that we would have a little extra breathing room. That our life would somehow be easier. The more negative we began feeling the more things started going wrong.

One day around this same time, I decided that I wanted to start making milk kefir (a fermented yogurt type drink). I had been making kombucha tea for years (a fermented tea drink) and heard about the added benefits of milk kefir. I posted in a milk kefir sharing group that I was looking to trade one of my SCOBY'S (kombucha tea mushroom) for milk kefir grains. To my surprise, I received a response immediately. I was so excited and a bit surprised that I had a response so quickly. The posting advises posters that it may take a few days even a few weeks to get a response. I scrambled to find something to ship the scoby in and when I went back to check my messages, I found that the person who wanted to trade had sent me six messages! I responded to her request giving her my mailing address and that I would ship her package on Monday. This was late on a Friday and I didn't want the package sitting in a warehouse all weekend. That next Monday, I arrived at work and logged into the site to let her know that I shipped the package to her that morning. She had been messaging me all weekend over and over, each message nastier and nastier. Her last message (there were about ten) stated that she canceled the shipment of my grains due to my lack of response. I messaged her one last time saying "thanks, but no thanks. I wanted a simple trade, nothing complicated and that her package did ship that morning as I had promised."

Five days later I decided to post another request. I was calmer, happier and my thoughts were much more relaxed and positive this time. That very same day I received a message from a very kind women offering local pick up since she also lived in Austin. When she asked if I lived near a certain landmark, I almost fell off my chair, I could not believe how perfect this was. She was just down the road from me. Within a day or two, we set up a time for me to pick up the grains. It could not have been any smoother. It was amazing to me, when I was chaotic and frazzled, I attracted a chaotic and frazzled person and situation. When I was happy, calm and appreciative that was who I attracted.

A few other things happened to me around this same crazed time. While driving Crosby to school one morning, I had an argument with a neighbor and bus driver at the entrance of our complex. When I arrived at work I shared this "outburst" with two of my coworkers. I realized what I was doing (drawing negative to me) so I decided not to share it with my husband until we were both at home that night, I did not want to throw any negative his way and cause negative in his day. I got myself under control as best I could and did not talk about it again, I let it go. That same week someone hit me in the school parking lot with NO damage to my vehicle at all, just a smudge mark. And the very next morning, I woke up to a flat tire. The tire just needed some fix a flat and I was on my way. I then realized that the negative feelings I had been attracting to me was the reason that all these little "annoyances" were occur-ring all at once.

It's funny because, around this same time, my husband and I were discussing how we were both feeling disappointed, upset, and a bit negative about not being where we intended to be at the "One Year" mark. And then it dawned on me, "WAIT!" "Who decided that we needed to be in a certain place at this point? We do not need to put any timeline on anything, it's up to us and only us, and we should not put that type of unnecessary pressure on us, we are doing great". We came with NOTHING and have so much, we have come so far in a year. We started then talking about everything we had accomplished in a year's time, instead of what we had not. After that, everything in our life became calmer and positive again, only good things came our way once again.

Reflections

How you feel is one of the most important indicators of what you are attracting to you, of what you are creating. Negative feelings can bring only negative outcomes. Those negative feelings are your warning light, your check engine light. It's your indicator that what you are creating is not good. When you notice this, stop immediately and search for a happy good feeling thought. When you find that happy thought, and it feels good, milk it. Milk those feel good feelings, think those dreamy, happy thoughts. Feel it. Soothe in it. Savor in it, knowing that just by changing your thoughts you are changing your outcome. Keep thinking and daydreaming, those thoughts. When you feel happy first, when you can feel happy and be positive first, then you are creating what you want.

Decide with each new day that you will not accept any other feelings but good feelings, happy thoughts and watch your life transform. Be calm, but firm. Ask yourself how are you feeling? Train yourself to flip it around. Feel good first, be happy first, and love yourself first, and watch everything in your life become magical.

8

Wishing Well

If you can dream it, YOU CAN do it

~Walt Disney

Each one of us has our very own personal wishing well. It's as big as an ocean, as calm and gentle as a slow moving stream, as abundant and full as all the stars in the Universe and as alive as a baby in a mother's womb.

Everything that you have EVER wanted, desired and wished for, has already been given to you. It has all been given to you immediately upon your asking and has been placed in your wishing well. Everything in your well is alive and waiting to be born. It's yours for eternity. Just as an unborn baby is real, alive, and, with nurture and care, will be born, so is everything in your well. Everything that you have ever wanted, wished for, dreamed of. Every thought you have thought, has been granted, it is real, it exists and is in your wishing well.

We are non-physical energy having a physical human experience. Our wishing well is in the non-physical. Remember, we are more non-physical than we are physical. It's real, but you must, without a doubt, know it. *It's a knowing, a faith.* It's a feeling in your gut, you just... Know. Knowing that it's real, believing in it, feeling it, is what will bring it to you into the physical. When you know, deep down, that what you have created is real, you begin to relax, you become calm and an overall sense of peace comes over you. You know that your desire has already been given to you. You know that it is done, you know that it is yours and that there is nothing more for you to do. Think of a pregnant women, especially before pregnancy tests, sonograms, and ultrasounds. She knew she was pregnant before she saw any signs. Then, as the weeks and months went on, she began to see signs, feel signs, she knew without a doubt that she was carrying a baby without seeing it. Your wishes and desires work the same way. You are pregnant with all your wishes.

Smaller things will just come easier to you at first, not because they are smaller but because it is easier for you to believe in them. The bigger things are just as simple to create but it's our beliefs that it's big so it must take longer. Or it's going to be harder to create or that you really don't believe that it's really possible. It's how WE think about the size of the wish that determines how fast we will manifest it.

As you begin creating your life on purpose, the small things will at first come much easier to you. But, what will happen is, with each new creation, you will start to believe in yourself a bit more, begin to believe that more is possible for you. You will be able to see your power more and your creations will begin to get bigger and bigger. Remember, you are God of your own life. Know this, feel this, and nothing but what you want can and will come to you. It is done, it is yours. It is in your wishing well. Knowing that you are deserving of everything you want and very powerful, will bring it to you. Your knowing will stop *your* resistance, you are the only one who is keeping it from coming to you.

When you know that you are deserving of everything you want, that you are very powerful, when you feel it, that gut feeling, knowing that it's revealing itself to you. That knowing, that faith, that is what will bring it to you. As you do this, the Universe will begin to show you signs. Just as a pregnant mother begins to see and feel signs of her impending motherhood, you will begin to see and feel signs before the actual birth of what you have asked for. They maybe just little impulses to go somewhere, do something, or you may see something on TV, hear something on the radio, or you'll over hear a conversation, someone may be talking about the very same thing you have been thinking about, wanting. Something will spark you to do something, to take action. Synchronicities and coincidences may happen, things that seem so bizarre will begin to take place. People you need will just appear before you (remember the HR Director I met?!). Ideas will just come to you, opportunities will flow AND all of it will happen with ease and calmness. Without much effort, pushing or stress of any kind. Without much work on your part, it will just become, come together, the universe will deliver it to you. Try it for yourself, think of a song, an object, a person, or a certain color car, anything. Tell the Universe and ask that you see it within 48hrs. Watch and wait with happy, light-hearted anticipation.

I witnessed a group of people on Facebook intend to manifest a pink car. Within hours, hundreds of people began posting pictures of pink cars they saw all around them. Some were cars, some were trucks, some posted pictures of pictures of pink cars that they came across. Some even found Barbie cars and hot wheels that were pink. This went on for months. For some, it came very easily, but for others who were more resistant, it took longer (many actually posted their *complaints* to *not* seeing a pink car which made it take longer) but it was truly miracu-lous what they found. Some found a pink car within a week, some, a month. For me, I really wasn't trying, I was just witnessing but I didn't see any and did make a mental note of it. BUT one day, after the posts were all done and the group moved on to manifesting money... That day, I was running on the treadmill. I looked out the window and I saw a truck that had a very large hot pink design on the front hood. Then just seconds later a bright bubblegum pink Volkswagen buggy drove by! Well that was by far the most impressive and miraculous one of all. I couldn't believe what I had just seen. I was still blown away with the first two I had just witnessed when I turned around and there was a very large magenta truck driving by. *It was all pink!* With a martini glass on the side! I was absolutely amazed, dumbfounded, shocked and speechless! I just could not believe that I had just witnessed three vehicles that were pink in less than five minutes! I love, love, love, this Life! Creating is so much fun!

My family and I had wanted to Leave Delaware for quite some time. With each passing year, we let everything that could get in our way. We let continuous obstacles stop us from moving forward (our focus point was on, we don't want to be in Delaware). We let so much control us that we were frozen in time (We kept focusing on the problem). Every year we said, "Ok definitely next year" but that next year came and went, something else getting in the way. One year it was my job loss, another, a car accident that totaled our vehicle. Another year we were too busy trying to finish renovating our house (it was gutted before I lost my job) but how do we pay to finish it? Thinking this way slowed us down. One year it was Hurricane Sandy that tore part of our roof off. Another it was a Disney vacation and a family wedding out of town. We let so much control us that we had no control. Until one day, we realized the boys were going to be in the seventh and eighth grade the following year. It was crunch time, it was now or never. If we were going to make this big move it would have to be the following year. It must be before Nolan started high school. Well, my first thoughts were, I wasn't keen on the idea of heading back to New York (where we had planned to go) after the bitter cold of the "Polar Vortex" (2012). The temperatures that winter were down in the single digits and we had snow storm after snow storm all winter long. The boys spent most of that winter home due to the snow. I had had enough of the cold, wanted nothing to do with cold weather snow or winter. At this point, we were no longer thinking about the "How". We stopped all that. We were now thinking of the "Where" (The solution). Where do we go? We had no vision of how we could make it happen. But what we did have was a knowing, we *knew* no matter what, we must be gone before September the following year.

Well, I cannot even begin to explain or express to you in words just how unbelievably easy and perfect the entire process from that very moment was. It was simply magical. As soon as we made the decision, drew the line in the sand, took the plunge, whatever we needed, everything and anything that we needed just came to us. We simply let go of the oars and drifted down stream. Everything just came to us in perfect synchronicity. And that's when the location appeared to us! It was Austin Texas! Wait! What? All of our family and friends were in NY. All that we have known was on the coast. We had never left the east coast let alone been to Texas. Why on earth would we move there? Well the Universe answered. It was as if Austin popped up everywhere we looked. Whatever we searched for, Austin was always one of the best places and top destinations. We searched The Best place to raise a family, best places for music, best places for holistic and green living, best weather, (if you like hot summers of course) most beautiful lakes, hiking trails, waterways, best Colleges, and Universities. We started noticing people talking about Austin, found signs, t-shirts, movies. Started meeting people who were either from Austin, had visited Austin or knew someone from Austin. Ok, we thought, Austin is where we need to be, but how?!?! How are we going to get there, it's over sixteen hundred miles away (1600). We had a house that was gutted and needed to be renovated, no money left in savings, how are we going to do this? Our credit was shot, we would need to find jobs! Oh! but what about the dogs? We didn't see a path. The only thing we did have was a want and a desire to make it happen.

In mid-2013 we set a time frame of September 2014 no matter what, that's when we leave. We decided even if we had to live in the van, we were going. Once we took this next step, once we made the final decision everything began to fall into place. We stopped thinking of the obstacles, stopped thinking of the "What-Ifs". We jumped, with both feet in. It was absolutely amazing how perfect everything came together. We found an apartment that was in the best school district that we could afford, in what most considered one of the best areas and most beautiful in Austin. We found a place to rent a trailer that was originally supposed to be twenty-five miles away from where we lived and instead, found one less than a mile away. The money we needed to get there just seemed to come to us from many different avenues, almost like falling out of the sky. The apartment we found was perfect, it was available the week that we needed, and in the perfect location (near stores, banks and schools.) with not one, but two pools, two hot tubs, a gym, media room, barbecue pits and they allowed two large dogs. Our Lease was approved even with our horrendous credit for a very affordable security deposit. We were thrilled and in complete shock. The vet bill for both dogs to get their shots was supposed to be $30, but we only paid $3! (A malfunction of the credit card machine) The weather on our drive could not have been more perfect, it was sunny and warm the whole way.

On our drive down, I remembered I had forgotten to set up a rental for a washer and dryer. Low and behold within minutes of me remembering this, I received a phone call from the apartment rental office. They called to tell me a washer and dryer had been left in the apartment by the previous tenant and they wanted to know if I wanted them! WOW! I was blown away! We arrived on a Monday, the boys were enrolled and started school on Wednesday. I had an interview on Friday and was working the following Monday. The very next week my husband was offered a job within walking distance of our apartment. Everything just unfolded in perfect synchronicity. It just could not have been any better, more perfect.

I really would like to stress to you that we literally left behind EVERYTHING. All we took with us was a 4x8 trailer of all our belongings. We sold or gave away 95% of all our stuff. We brought with us five dishes, four bowls, three pots and silverware for our kitchen. We had only beds for the boys and no other furniture. We sat on the floor for our first Thanksgiving and Christmas. But we did it. We made that impossible journey with such little effort and with miraculous events and outcomes.

Reflections

Each one of us has our very own personal wishing well. Everything that you have EVER wanted, desired and wished for, has already been given to you. It has all been given to you, placed in your wishing well and is waiting to be born. Your wishing well is in the non-physical. Everything in your well is alive and waiting to be born. It's real. It's a knowing. A faith. A gut feeling. You know without a doubt. YOU Just... KNOW. Knowing that it's real, believing in it, feeling it, is what will bring it to you into the physical. When you realize that what you have created is real, you begin to relax, you become calm and an overall sense of peace comes over you. When you have faith, peace, calmness, no doubt, that's when the Universe can deliver it to you.

As you begin creating your life on purpose, smaller things will just come easier to you at first. Not because they are smaller but because it is easier for you to believe them. The bigger things are just as simple to create but it's our beliefs that it's big so it must take longer, or it's going to be harder to create or that you really don't believe that it's truly possible. With each new creation though, you will start to believe in yourself more, start to believe that more is possible for you. You will "get it" understand it a little more each day. You will have a deeper knowing with each new creation. Remember, you are God of your own life. Know this, feel this, and nothing but what you want to manifest can and will come to you. It is done, it is yours. Be calm and at peace with it.

9

Ask and it is Given-
The Power in You

Ask, and it shall be given you; Seek, and ye shall find; Knock, and it shall be opened unto you.

~Matthew 7:7

According to the Law of Attraction, there are three steps in the creative process.

1. **Ask**
2. **Believe**
3. **Receive**

Step 1 Ask – It's what we do all day every day, we ask for what we want. When you see what you want, you ask (or pray for it). When you see what you *do not* want, you automatically know what you do want and you ask. This step is not something that you need to learn. You do this all day, everyday. What you need to realize though, is that whatever you have asked for, has been given to you in the moment that you asked. It is given to you and put into your wishing well.

Step 2 Believe – The Universe has answered, its job is done. Your wish has been granted. Whatever the problem was, the solution has been given. Whatever you have asked for, wanted and desired, has been given to you, Period... But, here's the rub in all of this; *you must not focus on the problem any longer in order to get to this step*. This step is where many get tripped up. Especially when it's something that you have a strong desire for and/or if you have been wanting it for a long time. OR if you don't really, truly believe you are worthy and deserving of it, if you doubt it's possible. What people tend to do instead is go right back to step #1 and ask again, over and over and over again. Make sense?

You must look for the outcome, the solution, the answer. You must work on seeing the signs, feeling it come to you. Remember you are already pregnant with your new desire as soon as you ask. *Know* that it's real. *Let go* of any doubt and it is yours.

Step 3 Receive – When you reach step 3, You know without a doubt that what you have asked for, wished for has been granted, you *know* it's coming. You feel it in your gut, you just... know. You have an attitude of faith; you know that it's yours, you are calm and happy. You know that you will see it soon. You are no longer stressed or worried. You let it go and trust that the

Universe will show it to you. You feel completely blessed, calm, tranquil and loved. You feel the Universe wrapping its arms around you. You feel the Unconditional Love, pouring out and to you. You know it's yours and in your wishing well, you know it's real. Feel the freedom.

Once you begin practicing these steps on a daily basis, begin creating your life on purpose, you will notice yourself getting really good at practicing and controlling the process, you will "get it". You will begin to notice a deeper understanding of who you really are and what this life really is. After a while, creating your life on purpose will become second nature to you. You will begin to notice a stronger and deeper knowledge. You will notice things will begin to come easier to you. You will see how your thoughts are becoming things in your own life. After you are manifesting your desires for quite some time you will have a better knowing of your powers. You will *know* your Thoughts are Alive, know that you are a Powerful Creator. You will, at this point understand how this all works.

As time goes on you will develop a mastery of the creation process. You will have gotten so good at step 3 that you will revel in it. You will feel happy all the time and know without a doubt how much the Universe loves you. Negativity won't bother you; you know at this point that it's part of life, that it helps you know what you do want. Everything will then come to you easily.

Eventually, you will reach a level that is a more powerful, more profound, a deeper, stronger knowing. You will know when you have reached this step that negativity serves you. You will know it helps you search and decide what you want next. Not only will it not bother you, but you will actually enjoy the negative. Knowing how necessary it is, that it helps you to focus. You will know how worthy and loved you are, that you are *Everything*. Nothing will ever bother you, you will be on top of the world. Knowing that this is all for you. You have mastered your ability to focus. You are a manifesting master! You are calm, peaceful, tranquil and full of Love for everyone.

We are ALL ONE, We are All FREE. If you have been successful in your life then you have used the Law of Attraction to your advantage possibly without ever knowing it. You were focused on what you wanted and determined to be successful. You knew what you wanted was yours, knew you would not take NO for an answer. That nothing could get in the way, nothing could stop you. You never doubted that you could have it. There was no wavering, you knew.

Now if you are on the other end of the spectrum and have experienced lack, illness or anything negative or painful in your life, it's ok. Just know that you are in control now, you can create intentionally now. You Now Can Create Positive Life Experiences Starting **Today**. Remember you are non-physical energy having a physical experience. You will always exist and you will always create. Be easy on yourself. Take it one day at a time. Focus on what you want, and be calm. Love yourself and be Happy first! EVERYTHING ALWAYS WORKS OUT FOR YOU.

Many years ago, shortly after we were first married, we had a car that needed engine work. We didn't have the money to fix it so we left it parked and we used one vehicle for quite a while. We had hoped to get it fixed because we were planning on moving and needed it to run.

The day that we were moving from New York to Delaware (a five and a half hour drive) is the day we started it. It had not been started for nearly six months. It started right up but with black plumes of smoke coming out of the exhaust. We put two quarts of oil in it, and packed it to the rim with boxes and our vacuum. I was so overly concerned that it wouldn't make it the whole trip. My husband, on the other hand, didn't seem to be bothered by it at all. He said, "if it breaks down, that's where we'll leave it." I freaked out, was overcome by fear! What?!?! But it's full of boxes and THE VACUUM! My car was also packed full, not a spot was left for anything. And if he broke down I would not have room for him either! NO! IT HAD TO MAKE IT!!! He drove in front of me, me behind, driving as close to him as I could, my knuckles white from holding onto the steering wheel so tight. Not letting any car get in between us. Each time we had to stop at a rest stop he put another quart of oil in and after a few attempts it would start back up. Whenever we had to stop to pay a toll (yes, this was long before EZ Pass and Toll Roads) It would stall and I would muster up this energy START, START, START!!!!!! YOU MUST START!!!! Overwhelming relief came over me when it finally started. With each stop we made, it was the same process. As we drove out of New York, we drove over bridges, up hills, each time the engine started to lose gusto, it would hesitate and putt-putt-putt, sounding as if it was going to stall. It would sputter, crawling, and then, slowly, barely moving, going only twenty miles per hour, it would pick up speed again, slowly at first and then faster and faster it would roll down the hill. OH THANK YOU, GOD!!! I yelled out loud each time. It was like this the entire trip. Each time taking longer to start, but it started each time. Each time an obnoxious black cloud of smoke poured out. I will never, ever forget the overwhelming, strong, powerful determination I felt that the car start, that it make it. About seven and a half hours later, as we pulled around the corner into the development, my fear began to dissipate a little. I began thinking, "well ok, at this point, if it stalls, we can push it from here, but Oh GOD! Just a little bit more!" And the most unbelievable, amazing, mind-boggling thing happened. As he pulled into the driveway, pulled into the parking spot I let out a sigh of relief and as I did, the engine let out a sputtering sound and died! Right there in the driveway. It never started again. But it made it. It made it all the way from New York to Delaware like I wanted, like I affirmed, like I demanded needed to happen. Now, I really have no idea if it was, in fact, my overwhelming desire and demanding, determined feelings and focus that it make it the whole way. Or if it was my husband's blasé-ness that it didn't matter one way or another. But, it did make it and died right in the spot.

Reflections

There are three steps in the creative process.

Step 1 Ask – This step does not require us to learn anything. We are such great creators, without even knowing it. We ask all day every day for what we want. When we are feeling negative, in our unhappy thoughts and unhappy feelings, when we are getting what we don't want, we automatically know and again ask for what we do want. It is given to you in the moment you ask and put into your wishing well.

Step 2 Believe – This step is not your job, it is the Universe's job. Your wish has been granted, the Universe has given it to you, you just don't choose how. Look for the signs. Look for the answer, the solution. Know that it is real and that it is done.

Step 3 Receive –When you reach this step, you are no longer stressed or worried. You have an attitude of faith. You feel the love from the Universe, you know your worthiness, you know how blessed you are and you know without a doubt, that what you have asked for is on its way. You just know.

Once you have practiced for awhile you will have a better, deeper Knowing. A stronger depth of the mastery of the creative process. You know it's a part of life. You know and see that everything comes to you easily. Eventually, you will reach a level of knowing that negativity serves you. It helps you decide what you want next. You will enjoy the negativity and know how imperative it is in your creation process. Nothing will bother you, you are on top of the world, on cloud 9. You have mastered the creative process.

10

Remote Control - You Hold The Power

If you correct your mind, the rest of your life will fall into place.

~Lao Tzu

Let me first start out by saying that we are all human. Be calm and easy with yourself. Take this new knowledge (that you are just learning), one day at a time. We have all been programmed generation after generation after generation that we need to work hard, suffer and endure to get through life. That we don't get anywhere without it. That, this life, is somehow a test. And, if we are good and work hard and suffer enough, we will have a spot in the Promised Land.

We do not have to struggle or suffer. Nothing could be further from the truth. We do not have to work hard. Actually, that's what's been keeping us from getting what we want and desire more easily. Everything that you have asked for has been given to you. If you feel doubt or worry about it, if you do not believe it is possible, then you have to find a way to feel it. You have to find a way to be positive, to believe it and know that *it has been given* to you in order for you to receive it. It is the only way! Like a radio frequency our thoughts are wavelengths, electromagnetic fields. Each thought has its own frequency, each question has its own frequency and each answer a different one from the question. One of the best processes for me to get a better understanding of this has been to picture myself with a remote control. It's my controller, it's in my hand. It's in my possession, and I hold all the power.

Think of a television station. You have to change the channel (the frequency) to that TV station to see the show you want to see. No matter what you do or who you are, you will not be able to see a show that's on channel 31 if you are on channel 13, it's the wrong frequency and will never broadcast or be seen by you. You get this, you understand this concept. It's the same exact concept when it comes to us receiving what we have asked for. If we are on a different channel or looking (focusing) on the problem and not the solution then it's the wrong channel. The wrong station for what you are asking for. You must change the channel in order for you to be on the right frequency. The way you do this is by making the decision that it's done. When we are tense and pushing, prodding to get the work done, we are actually doing ourselves a disadvantage. The struggle, the pushing against the grain is what's keeping what you want away from you. With YOUR remote, you can now guide, direct it to what you want to see. Know that you are in control, and that it is yours. Receiving what you want is just as easy as changing the channel. Change the channel from the not having it station to the having it station. Once you change the station, you then are saying yes to whatever it is you are asking for, you are letting it in. You're on the wrong channel when you are complaining, focusing on the problem, undecided what to do next. BUT the Very moment you make the decision, you decide your next step, take the leap, when you "know," that is when you change the channel, and now you are on the right channel!

Be easy, let it come to you. You know that you are powerful and deserving of what you are asking for. Take the forcing of it out and instead, let go. Picture yourself in a canoe flowing down a calm stream, see yourself let go of the oars, and let the stream take you along. You are receiving what you have asked for. Know this. Feel the calm, happiness and love inside of you. Feel the excited anticipation of it, be peaceful, loving, tranquil, free. Know that it is yours, that everything always works out for you. It's really that simple.

One day while at work, my husband called me and told me that our van wouldn't start. We were only in Austin about a month so we really didn't know anyone or where to go to fix it. "No big deal" he said, he would find someone to give his battery a jump and we would take the battery on our day off to have it checked. The battery was only about 6 months old, we knew it wasn't a big deal. When I got home (I got a ride home from a co-worker) he called me again, said that the jump didn't work, the van still wouldn't start and that one of his co-workers was going to take him to have the battery checked. OK no big deal, surprising to me, we were both very calm about it. I kept saying out loud how strange the whole thing was. "It's ok, it will all work out" he said to me. He texted me about an hour later, saying the battery was fine and a group of co-workers was now standing around him, each with their tools in hand, one by one trying to dissect the problem. He and I decided it was best to call a tow truck (the solution). We still remained calm, still thinking how strange this all was and peaceful all at the same time, we were not worrying or panicking. I called our insurance company. They were going to have a tow truck go to his job and pick up the van free of charge since we have towing coverage on our policy. Ahh, ok everything is ok. The rep told me they have only one company nearby that they are contracted with and it was closer to his job, but about ten miles to our apartment. I explained our situation; we just moved in from the east coast, we both have new jobs, only one vehicle at the moment and he was stranded at work. I was at home about fifteen miles away. I asked if there was any way to have the van towed to the shop just behind us. That would be the most convenient since he could walk home from there. She explained to me that she had to map it within closest range to where he was at. Oh boy. She was able to work with me a bit and found another location only 3 miles away from our apartment, something about a one time courtesy something. Since it's closer to our home instead of his work. OK, so now I still need to find some way to get us to work tomorrow. He texted me that a friend was going to drive him home. I found a car rental place that would pick us up the next morning and the insurance company would pick up most of the tab. Wow, I thought, this is all working out. Except, at the very moment I hung up with the car rental place my husband texted me again, saying that he was with the tow truck driver since he is towing the van to the place behind us. What?!?!? UH-OH, that's not where he is bringing you! I guess the location of where they were bringing the van got lost in our texting communication. So I calmly let him know where he was headed and that I would try to get a ride to pick him up. I called a neighbor/coworker I had just met and asked if there is any way she could drive me to get him when he arrives (twenty minutes later), she agreed. The whole time though we were both so calm and everything was flowing well. A few little hiccups but all was well. I got one last call and this time It was my husband telling me to have one of the boys come down NOW, in our parking lot with my key! What?!!? What's going on!? He told me he figured out what was wrong, and explained it to the tow truck driver. After hearing our plight, the driver decided to drop him off here at the apartment so he could try my key. My husband figured it out! It was not the battery or anything else, it was the key! We had been having issues with his key and since mine was in brand new condition and working well he knew it would work. So we all ran out and while the van was still on the tow bed the driver got in and tried my key and to our delight it started right up! OMG! We were just in absolute amazement, we remained calm, continued focusing on the solution, stayed positive, and everything worked out perfectly. It could not have worked out better. Not only did everyone come to our aid, but both my husband and van were delivered to me at my front door all free of charge!

We didn't know it then, but the Universe was working in our favor through the whole ordeal.

Reflections

We have all been programmed generation after generation that we have to work hard in this life in order to get results. No pain, no gain. This simply is not true. Everything that we have ever asked for has been given to us. If we doubt it, don't believe it, or feel negative about it, we can't receive it. BUT, when we know and understand our Power and know without a doubt that it is ours, we get it, every time. In order for us to receive it though, we must be able to line up with it. You must be calm. It's a knowing in your mind, in your gut. Just like a knowing that you are on the wrong channel when you want to see a TV show. Picture yourself with a remote controller. When you don't feel like you have received what you have asked for then change the channel from NOT having it to the having it channel. Just be calm about it, peaceful, loving and know that it is yours, that it *always* works out for you. It's that simple.

11

Your Inner Self

There is a voice that doesn't use words. LISTEN

~ Rumi

Have you ever talked to yourself (of course you have, we all have) and felt as though you just received a response? You immediately got some type of inspiration to go somewhere or do something? Or immediately the phone rang and the answer is on the other end of the phone? Or maybe you simply felt in your gut that someone was with you, answering your wishes and keeping you safe. It's your Inner Self you are feeling. Our inner self is always with us. It's the voice in your head. It's your guidance system, your guardian angel, your connection. Your inner self is the FULL non-physical part of you. It's what we call our Soul, our Spirit. It's that inner voice you hear. It's the whole of you, the ALL of you. It's that gut instinct. It's the bigger part of you. you can always trust it, *it's you.* When we die, our inner self is the part of us that goes on. It's only our body that dies, the physical part of us. The rest of us, the "Most" of us, the larger part of us, goes on forever. We are eternal, we are consciousness, we are Energy in

Human Form. Feel the Happiness of your Inner self, feel the Love. You are an Infinite Being.

Allow your inner self to be your Universal Manager. When you allow it to, it will delegate your wishes, your wants, your desires. Allow it to take care of and manage it all for you. I think of my Inner self as my twin, my Big twin who is also my best friend. Your inner self knows who you truly are, always has your back and never doubts your intentions. It knows how worthy you are. Knows how powerful, perfect you are and always Loves You, Unconditionally. When you have negative feelings or any doubt, your inner self immediately lets you know you are not on the right channel to receive your wish. Your inner self will give you feedback whether that thought is in line with your desire or not. It's the guidance within you, helping you mold the energy of your wish, with your feelings, helping you to connect and adjust your point of focus. Guiding you to the path of your desire. You can feel it in your gut. You have a spiritual entourage always with you, always surrounding you. Allow it to be. Your inner self is always celebrating your every step in all of your life adventures, fully seeing the miracle of you. You are a Legend! Feel the unconditional Love! Feel Your Power! Your inner self will guide you to the rest. Your goal is to feel good, feel peaceful, calm. Be happy, and joyful. Feel safe, be safe! YOU ARE A BEAUTIFUL SOUL!

There are many back roads I use to drive on in Delaware, to avoid the "beach traffic" in the summer. One late night while leaving work, I turned on a back road and drove for a few miles. All of a sudden, this overwhelming feeling of fear and dread came over me. I had no idea why, but I began to slow down on the winding dark road I was on. I slowed and slowed till I was at a crawl, still the fear and uneasiness consuming me. It felt as if something was whispering in my ear to stop. I stopped, dead in the middle of the road and at that very moment, I saw a whole family of deer run right in front of me. Not just one or two. No! It was three or four very large males, a few females, and even a few smaller ones. There were seven or eight in total! They ran almost single file darting across the street. I could not believe what I was witnessing. If I had not stopped I would have been involved in a pretty serious accident. I did not realize it at that moment, but I now know without a doubt that it was my Inner Self in my ear that night. My inner self was warning me to slow down, to turn around, keeping me safe. I am so glad I listened.

Reflections

Your inner self is the full non-physical part of you. It's what we call our Soul. It's that inner voice you hear. It's the whole part of you. Your guardian angel. Your inner self communicates to you. That gut feeling you get, that's your inner self , it's you. It's always there to help you, guiding you to the path of your wishes. It's there helping you mold the energy and, with your feelings, helping you to connect and to adjust your point of focus. You have a spiritual entourage always with you, always surrounding you. Always celebrating your every step in all of your life adventures. Fully seeing the miracle of you, loving you unconditionally. It will never steer you wrong. Feel the Love! When you allow it, it will flow to you. The Universe loves you unconditionally. Your goal is to feel good, be happy, calm, peaceful and joyful. Feel safe, be safe!

12

Thought Power

The Spirit of the individual is determined by his dominating thought habits

~ Bruce Lee

Our thoughts are Energy. Think of electricity. Have you ever touched an outlet cord that may have been frayed and got a little jolt that ran up your elbow? It freaks you out, it's just enough energy to make you jump, but not enough to harm you. Now think of a strong bolt of lightning. Same energy, one is just extremely more powerful and will have a much more severe impact.

Your thoughts are exactly the same way. *Your Thoughts are Electric.* One thought, either positive or negative doesn't have much power. It's not going to move your world. But, when you think of one thought and then another thought builds upon it and another (LOA- like attracts like) you begin to build momentum, the power gets much more intense. It gets bigger, stronger, and more powerful. With just four similar thoughts, fifteen seconds each, a minute later, boom, creation begins. Now, what you created in that moment completely depends on if it was positive or negative. However, you just took a group or cluster of thoughts and made a reality. It's real. Know it, believe it, feel it, live it.

Try and think of a time when you got angry at someone or a situation. It was one thought, one comment, one thing that happened. Within seconds, another thought, (or comment) and then another. After just a minute or two, steam was coming out of your ears, maybe you yelled, screamed, cursed, maybe you hit something. It became harder to calm down, to let it go. Maybe a fight ensued. You may have said or done something you really didn't mean to.

On the other hand, can you think of a time when someone gave you a compliment or said something positive, something kind? Gave you a gift or a kind gesture, something loving? A smile appeared on your face, you then returned a positive comment. You were smiling from ear to ear, smiling so hard you felt it down in your gut. Within just a minute or two you were gushing over that person. Feeling joyous, happy, loved, appreciated and tickled pink, it made your day. You felt on top of the world and maybe possibly, you may have even started crying for joy! You felt special, significant and loved. You probably wanted to reciprocate that wonderful gift or gesture.

We are electricity, our thoughts really are that powerful! The great thing about knowing this, now you have control. You are holding the remote and now control the direction of your thoughts. If it starts to feel negative in any way, STOP! If it feels uncomfortable, STOP! Clear it out of your mind with something, anything that is positive. It can be as simple as, I love my dog. There that just changed the direction. Now build on it. I love my dog because he does silly things that make me laugh. Ok. 2. Now expand on it, and build up the momentum. I love my dog because he loves taking rides with me in my car. 3 and we have fun playing catch at the dog park, 4. Now you feel that love, feel happy and positive. You can now start thinking positive thoughts that are closer in the direction of what you are wanting to create now. Sometimes it's just a better process to find something off the subject completely when you are trying to turn around negative thoughts. But, it must be done as soon as you realize you're thinking a negative thought. You Do NOT want to create in that moment.

Let's face it though we are human, even having a strong grasp of this for a lifetime, we will still find from time to time that we fall in the negative category. Emotions, bad days, unwanted things, whatever. But now, you can begin to look at it all differently. As soon as you know what you don't want, you immediately know what you do want. When something negative shows up at your front door that you do not want, in that very moment you know instantly what it is that you do want, precisely in that moment. When a large bill comes in immediately you want money to pay it. When you are hungry you want food, when you are sick you want wellness, when you fall down you want to get back up. When something breaks you want it fixed or replaced. When you are sad, you want happiness When you're lonely you want a companion. It's that un-wanting, that makes you ask for something new. It's life, even negative feelings are feelings, you came here for them. You came to expand, to create, to feel. With each new asking, you grow, you build upon what you have already created but now you can create on purpose. You are now in control, you now hold all the Power. You are FREE! You don't have to spiral out of control ever again.

The headlight went out on my car, it was a fairly new vehicle, it had less than fifteen thousand miles on it, so we took it to the dealer since it should fall under the warranty. After sitting at the dealership for hours we found out that it was not covered and that it would cost $450 to replace the headlight because the "new" cars now require that you replace the whole assembly. Which in laymen's terms means, the whole entire head lamp needs to be replaced. The whole thing, not just the bulb. Seriously?!?!? Well, since it was early spring I decided that I could buy myself some time since the days were growing longer and I really wouldn't need to use my lights too often till the fall and when in the rare case I did, I would just use my bright lights. My husband mentioned to me that the registration was due April 1st but for some reason it just didn't register with me what he was trying to say to me (in one ear out the other.) Fast forward to June and I decided I better register the car... I went to the DMV website and found that it must be inspected first. OK, so I was about to make an appointment to bring it in to get inspected and my husband said to me, "it's not going to pass, you need to fix the headlight." OH CRAP! I don't know why I didn't put two and two together. I really wasn't sure what I was thinking. Ok, so I will do it in a few weeks when I get up the money.

One night that week while lying in bed, Out of the blue, I began to get this vision of a police officer pulling me over. OH MY GOD!!! I tried really hard to stop it and think a new thought! I knew in that moment I was creating my future, it felt so real. I literally envisioned sitting in my car and a police officer standing at my window. I needed to stop that thought NOW!!! "OK Cindy, think a new thought, now!" Thinking happy, loving thoughts, completely off the subject worked...

The next morning as I got into my car to drive to work I kept saying to myself, "I am safe, I am in my little bubble, I am safe" and I envisioned myself pulling into the parking lot at work. I did this for weeks! Some days I felt a bit fearful and instantly bam, there was a cop. Each time though, they were either too far away to notice my expired sticker or pulling someone else over. It was amazing to me how many I started to see. They were there, all around me, near me, but never close enough. Each time I saw them, I said out loud "I am safe" "thank you for keeping me safe!" And they would drive in the opposite direction, away from me. Each day I knew it was my thoughts, my energy bringing them in my view or not. Each day I could see how the way I was feeling, created exactly how I felt right in front of my eyes. It was truly remarkable to see my energy at work. Some days I was calm, had no fears about it or simply forgot to worry. On those days I never saw any police. Other days I had some fear, worry in me and there they were, popping up out of nowhere.

The first few weeks after I had the headlight replaced, and registered the car, I still saw a few cops near me. However, since I was "legal" I had no further resistance to them, it was fine that they drove near me. It was fine if they were next to me, it no longer mattered and within the first few days I hardly noticed any police at all. Truly, truly remarkable.

Reflections

Our thoughts are energy, they are electric. Just like electricity, one thought is not all that powerful. But, when one thought builds upon it and another, the power gets much more intense. It gets bigger, stronger, and more powerful. We are electricity, our thoughts really are that powerful! The great thing about knowing this, now you have control. You are holding the remote and now control the direction of your thoughts. It can be as simple as focusing your thoughts on a completely different subject and thinking how happy it makes you. You are now in control of your life, you have all the power to create your life on purpose. You can guide your thoughts to where you want them to go. You can guide them away from any and all negative thoughts. You control it ALL! You don't have to live in fear or be afraid of negative situations ever again!

13
Happiness Matters!

Live Life as if Everything is rigged in your favor
~Rumi

Your Happiness is one of the most important feelings you will ever have. Happiness is THE answer. I know I have said this, stressed this throughout this book. My hope is that you will go deeper and get a more profound understanding of how this all works, what this means for you and your life. It's what we are all seeking. This IS where your Freedom lies. Your days should begin Happy, Every day! Be Happy and what you want will come to you. Whatever you want, now or in your future no matter what it is that you want, it is because you know that having it will make you happy. It's the feeling of happiness that you are seeking. Anything that you ever want, is because you know it will make you feel happy, feel good, feel joyous. That's why you want it. BUT remember, you have to feel Happy (Positive) in order to get what you want. So you must be Happy First. No matter what is going on in your life right now, you must **Get Happy**. Nothing will change in your life until you begin to focus on happiness. Feel good, be happy, feel it down in your gut. Accept nothing else other than how you feel as priority. Once you do this, then there is nothing that you cannot have or be or do. Nothing! You are flipping around (one hundred eighty degrees) everything you were ever taught, have known and have lived. Please remember, what you are seeing and experiencing in your life right now are the results from your past thoughts. What you are thinking right now is creating your future. Do not stay in that place of anything in your life that you do not want any longer. Your only focus, from this point forward, is to feel good while being easy on yourself. Be calm and pay attention to how you feel. Your thoughts are Alive. You are the creator of your life. You hold all the Power, you can now create your life on purpose. Think about your wishes and desires, and mold those thoughts into your creation. Guide it the way you want it to be, not how it is or how you think it will be or can be. Shape it and dream it HOW YOU WANT IT TO BE. Then, be sure to let it go! Relax, be calm and let it come to you. The Universe can only do this once you take this step.

Turn your back to anything unwanted. Start to think of positive outcomes, dreams, desires to make your future what you want it to be. Think it, mold it into being, see it, envision it how you want your life to be. Day by day, thought by thought you will begin to see the changes coming to you. You are the creator of your life, your reality, but you do this by thinking not by doing. It's the "doing" that slows things down. When you try and force something to happen, you get in the way of it flowing easily to you. Don't let yourself feel rushed or pressured. Don't let each new step in the right direction discourage you because you have not reached the top yet. Start at day one and take each new day in stride. Tell yourself, this is a new day and I get to choose how I feel. Give yourself a break. Feel Happy and with each new creation, each new day, know that it is just another step in your life, another wonderful happy day, a new adventure. Do not continue with the same story, change your story. This is a new way of living your life. This should not be looked at as a one time thing. Something to do to get the money or the relationship you want. This is your new life. Your new beautiful all in your control, life. Life is a playground, have fun and explore your world! Live your life with ease, magic, fun! With each new day build upon the last and let your creations be even more amazing. This is the creative process. Be easy on yourself, you don't have to get there today.

Be sure to Celebrate each new milestone, no matter how small you think it may be, celebrate each step you take up the flight of stairs, celebrate each step you take on your new path!

Take a moment to take a deep breath and relax. Begin today with a fresh new start, a clean slate, a whole new day to create your Best Day Ever! Your goal should be to Love your life so much that you wake up *Everyday* happy, excited and awestruck. Cheering on another glorious day you get to play and create, here on this Earth. After all, shouldn't that be the reason to be Alive?!

Your "re-training" or "re-membering" started as soon as you picked up this book. The hard part is over, the stress is over. *You Now Know Your Truth.* You know how it all works. It only gets better from here. You are now in control, you are FREE! Be easy with yourself. Take it one day at a time and know there is nothing that you need to "study" you know what to do, you know and understand. Your work is to not be "lazy" and let your mind wander. Your work is to flip around, guide your thoughts when you get negative, it's not to push or force anything.

When you look at anything in nature it just flows. Slowly sometimes, fast at other times but there is a natural feel to it all. Everything in life did not happen overnight. Trees, grass, plants, they do not strain or rush to grow, but do it with ease and without force. Anything that was ever created took time. Anything in nature is never rushed. Animals, bodies of water, plants, they are all alive, moving, growing, living, being. They are doing it with ease, no stress or strain, but with power. Picture a plant emerging through the pavement in a parking lot, or a tree growing around or through an object. Nothing is impossible and nothing is too hard. Even our breathing is done with ease. Our breathing happens without us consciously breathing. Our nails and hair grow, without our "doing anything" and they do it with calmness, easiness. We do not have to think about it or make it happen. The blood flows through our veins and our organs move and pump without us. The only things that are forced, pushed and rushed in this world are us. We humans need to re-learn how to be easier with our lives and let things flow more often. It's only humans who put pressure on things, force, rush and stress about things. Take a moment to breathe. Be calm and begin to mold your thoughts, guide them one by one to positive outcomes. Use your mind more to create and *less pushing to make things happen.* Envision how you want each outcome to be, change your thoughts to what you are wishing the outcome to be.

Picture yourself going up a staircase. You must take each step no matter how many there are fifty or fifty thousand. You can skip a few steps here and there, you can walk or run but you still have to pass each step, you still have to climb them. That staircase is your life adventures. With each new thought you take a step up to positive dreams, positive outcomes, and positive creations. Be easy and take it all one day at a time. Thought by thought, day by day, each outcome, each day will end positively and each day will be better than the last.

It's time for you to become fully aware of the power within you. For you to accept that you are a powerful creator. It's time for you to care about how you feel. To realize that how you feel matters. To know and understand that finding and holding onto good feelings, positive happy thoughts are important. That your thoughts and feelings are connected! You are royalty!

Life is a miracle. We often hear this, but we don't take the time to really think about, or comprehend what this really truly means. We don't question IF the sun will come up or IF the Earth will keep rotating and keep spinning in its orbit. IF the ocean waves will continue to crash and recede. But it does. Isn't that a miracle in and of itself? We don't question if there will be enough air to breathe today, but there is. Look out in nature, there are miracles everywhere.

We are Miracles too. So why not become conscious of this and become more aware. Take notice of the miracles around you. Become more calm, more peaceful. Be sure to always feel good, feel Happy every day. Start Every day feeling this way! Intend it today and every day. Begin a new routine. Decide when you go to sleep at night that you will start your day Happy. Have some type of plan in place. It can be as simple as an affirmation you say each day. Or if you are not usually a morning person and it takes a while to get moving in the morning then just take a few extra minutes to lay in bed and feel good. Feel the smoothness of your sheets, the comfort of your bed, and the warmth of your blanket. Feel happy and joyful for another day. Feel the peacefulness of the quiet morning (sorry if you have small kids this may not keep you feeling peaceful) Find whatever it is that DOES make you happy and think about it. Just take a few minutes before jumping out of bed and think about how lucky and miraculous you are and how your life truly is wonderful! Go through all the things that you are grateful for, all the things you have to be thankful. Feel the joy and happiness fill up in you. Try to NOT think about that thing that you do NOT want in your life. Create a new life, by forgetting about it for as long as you can. You can also begin your day writing how you want your day to go with as much detail as you can while feeling good. Read positive affirmations, listen to and watch positive videos or go outside in nature. Whatever fits in your day. Create a new schedule and make sure it's things that make you happy, positive and feeling good.

I hope with all my heart that you have truly grasped just how powerful and loved you are. The Universe Loves you unconditionally and always has your back. Now that you understand how life works and hold this knowledge in you to create your life on purpose, your life is already better for you today than yesterday.

When I was in sales, no matter what I was selling, no matter where I worked, I always used a script when I first started each new job, each new position, each new product I was selling. I usually received a standard script and I would re-word it to make it my own. If it sounded fake to me or if I didn't believe what I was saying, how was the person on the other end of the phone going to believe or trust me. So I constantly re-worked my script, making it "my own". And I got really good at it. I used my words, my flow and made sure that the essence of what I needed to say was never lost.

As you re-learn and re-create your life on purpose I highly recommend that you begin to create your own script. Plant the Happy Seed in your new garden and create your new life. It does not have to be complicated and it's not to sell others on what you have learned. It's to get you to have some type of footing to begin creating your new life with. Then little by little you will change it up, molding it to match your thoughts and feelings. As you get better and better at this, your ideas and creativity will grow. It will expand and your words will begin to have a deeper and more profound meaning.

So how about you start with something simple.

I am the creator of my world. I know this, I believe this. I feel this in my gut. My life is unfolding perfectly. I don't ever have to feel

rushed or stay in any negative feelings, emotions or situations. Every day I am planting new seeds, new seeds that are happy and positive. I am in control of my life and only good can come to me. Life is beautiful right here and right now. Everything always works out for me. I am love, I am happy! I am free! Life is easy, fun and magical!

Of course, you can add and delete anything that you do not feel comfortable with or if it isn't believable to you. Just be sure to keep it real and simple. Build on it often. Have fun with it.

Remember your thoughts are Alive, when you notice your thoughts becoming negative, you start feeling sad, anxious, fearful or angry. You now have the knowing to stop them right in their tracks. You can now control your thoughts and bring bigger and better life experiences, events, opportunities and adventures to you. Have Fun! And Love Life! I understand that this information can be overwhelming, I know that controlling your thoughts can sometimes be a challenge, but please, please be sure to keep it light and have fun with this along the way. Say to yourself every day, "things are getting better and better. Everything is coming easier and easier to me. Things always work out for me. I am Happy!" Laughter attracts Laughter and Happy attracts Happy! You deserve nothing but Happiness!

Get yourself a notebook or journal. Decorate it, make it your own. Call it your "Happiness Journal." Start writing in it every day, all of your wishes, desires, positive quotes, dreams, pictures, write about things you love, things you want to create, positive creations you want and wish for. Draw, write, write poetry, whatever makes you happy. Change your story, start writing your new story. Your life is yours to create. Play games to make it exciting and new. Make a vision board. Cut out and place on your board all the things you want to see in your life. Create adventures, play the positive what if game. What if, I ... you create it and have fun with it. Pick three things that you want the Universe to show you or bring to you. Have fun with it, be silly, and relax. Communicate with like-minded people and form study groups or Meet-Ups! Begin to intentionally create your life. The pen is in your hand!

Please take your time, go at your own pace. This is a personal journey. Never be afraid to create your own way, to take a different path. There are no right or wrong ways to create, there are thousands and thousands of them. You may be surprised to find that what you have been searching for all this time is completely different than what you thought you wanted.

I wish for your days to be full of fun and adventures. That you, wake up every morning happy to get another day on this beautiful planet and yell it out loud, Yay! Another day I get to play here on this Earth! Where you are excited to be Alive, and are absolutely in love with your life!

Be Calm, Be Peaceful, Be Love, Be Happy, Be easy, Be Free, Have Fun, Go on Adventures, Seek the Magic!

I do hope that you will send me emails telling me all of the delicious new Adventures, objects and life events you have created. I can't wait to hear all about them!

Email me at thoughtsalive@outlook.com

Facebook @thoughtsaliveyourpowertohappiness

Instagram lawofattraction_Thoughtsalive

Snapchat cindy thoughtsalive

Twitter @thought_alive

You are a Beautiful Soul! I hope you live a life you are head over heals in love with!!!

All My Love, <3 Cindy

For what it's worth; it's never too late to be whoever you want to be. I hope you live a life you're proud of, and if you find that you're not, I hope you find the strength to start over.

~ F. Scott Fitzgerald

13 Things to Always Remember

1.   The Universe doesn't hear what you are saying, it feels what you mean. It feels your feelings, your vibrations.

2.   Take it all one day at a time. There is no "catching up", no timeline, and no time clock. Just relax, breathe, and be peaceful!

3.   When you are intentionally creating, you know it. You feel it in your gut. You feel calm, happy, and peaceful. If you haven't reached these three feelings, you are not creating what you want.

4.   You never stop learning this, there is no end. When I started writing this book it was because I had it all figured out and wanted to share this with the world. Little did I know, by writing this book I have a much more profound understanding. I now "see" how this works, when before I just "got it." I now know that this knowledge I have, is just the tip of the iceberg. I will never know it all. I will always be the teacher as well as the student, BUT I will also not ever again NOT know this information as well. Think of it as a leveling up. You cannot go backwards, you keep moving forward, never forgetting but never reaching the end.

5.   Be sure to always be calm enough, peaceful enough to hear your inner self . Remember your inner self IS YOU! No one else would have your back more than you!

6.   Remember your Wishing Well is full of everything you have ever asked for. Everything starts in the non-physical. Know it, feel it in your gut! Relax, let go and it will come to you, It's real!

7.   You hold all the power in your world, your life! You are the Queen or King of your life. Nothing can come near you, nothing can come into your life that you do not want to let in. You are loved, you are safe, you are magic, you are Royalty!

8.   Our thoughts really are Alive, they rule your world. We really are creators, we really are electric. We are energy! Go create what you want!

9.   Your thoughts build upon themselves. Building power, building energy, creating what you are thinking. Don't be lazy and let your thoughts get away from you! Take control, do the work. Your work is to change, to steer, your thoughts as soon as you feel any negative feelings, to what you want to see in your life, that is your one and only job.

10. Be happy first! Start your day, every day Happy! Nothing is more critical than feeling

good! Make a point to wake up Happy Every Single Day of Your Life! Have fun with it!

11.   Relax more, be easy, calm. Do not force anything to happen. Let it come to you.

12. Remember you are a Soul. A Beautiful Soul, there is nothing to ever fear. Ever! Find your Happiness, live the life that you desire. You can be happy, healthy and love your life!

13. You hold the remote! You are the creator of your life! Live the life of your dreams! THIS **IS** YOUR POWER TO HAPPINESS!

* Offering both individual and group coaching, email or go to <u>cindywahlberg.com</u> for more info.

Once you make a decision, the Universe Conspires to make it happen.

~ Ralph Waldo Emerson

If you enjoyed **Thoughts Alive** please take a few moments to post a review on Amazon.com or email it to the publisher at info@positive-imaging.com.

Thank You!